TIM LINCECUM

Mary Boone

Mitchell Lane

PUBLISHERS

P.O. Box 196
Hockessin, Delaware 19707
Visit us on the web: www.mitchelllane.com
Comments? email us: mitchelllane@mitchelllane.com

Printing   1   2   3   4   5   6   7   8   9

A Robbie Reader Biography

Abigail Breslin	Drake Bell & Josh Peck	LeBron James
Adrian Peterson	Dr. Seuss	Mia Hamm
Albert Einstein	Dwayne "The Rock" Johnson	Miley Cyrus
Albert Pujols	Dwyane Wade	Miranda Cosgrove
Alex Rodriguez	Dylan & Cole Sprouse	Philo Farnsworth
Aly and AJ	Eli Manning	Raven-Symoné
AnnaSophia Robb	Emily Osment	Roy Halladay
Amanda Bynes	Emma Watson	Selena Gomez
Ashley Tisdale	Hilary Duff	Shaquille O'Neal
Brenda Song	Jaden Smith	Story of Harley-Davidson
Brittany Murphy	Jamie Lynn Spears	Sue Bird
Charles Schulz	Jennette McCurdy	Syd Hoff
Chris Johnson	Jesse McCartney	Taylor Lautner
Cliff Lee	Jimmie Johnson	Tiki Barber
Dakota Fanning	Johnny Gruelle	**Tim Lincecum**
Dale Earnhardt Jr.	Jonas Brothers	Tom Brady
David Archuleta	Jordin Sparks	Tony Hawk
Demi Lovato	Justin Beiber	Troy Polamalu
Donovan McNabb	Keke Palmer	Victoria Justice
	Larry Fitzgerald	

Library of Congress Cataloging-in-Publication Data
Boone, Mary, 1963–
  Tim Lincecum / by Mary Boone.
     p. cm. — (A Robbie reader)
  Includes bibliographical references and index.
  ISBN 978-1-61228-058-5 (library bound)
  1. Lincecum, Tim, 1984– —Juvenile literature. 2. Baseball players—United States—Biography—Juvenile literature. 3. Pitchers (Baseball)—United States—Biography—Juvenile literature. I. Title.
  GV865.L535B66 2012
  796.357092—dc23
  [B]
                                                          2011016790
eBook ISBN: 9781612281704

ABOUT THE AUTHOR: Mary Boone has written more than 20 books for young readers, including Robbie Reader Biographies about baseball player David Wright and WNBA star Sue Bird. Mary, her husband, Mitch, and their kids, Eve and Eli, live in Tacoma, Washington, not far from the fields where Tim Lincecum first learned how to pitch.

PUBLISHER'S NOTE: The following story has been thoroughly researched and to the best of our knowledge represents a true story. While every possible effort has been made to ensure accuracy, the publisher will not assume liability for damages caused by inaccuracies in the data, and makes no warranty on the accuracy of the information contained herein. This story has not been authorized or endorsed by Tim Lincecum.

TABLE OF CONTENTS

Words in **bold** type can be found in the glossary.

Right-handed pitcher Tim Lincecum is known for his long stride and flailing limbs. His best pitches include a fastball that reaches 95 miles per hour, a slider, and a curveball.

Boy Wonder

Having just pitched the San Francisco Giants to the 2010 World Series title, Tim Lincecum (LIN-sih-kum) grasped the 30-pound silver trophy and announced to reporters: "It's shiny."

Coming from Lincecum, that odd and obvious statement didn't seem all that odd and obvious. Almost everything about him is unusual: At 5 feet 11 inches tall and 165 pounds, he's shorter and slimmer than most professional pitchers. In the dugout, he hides under a towel. With his knit cap pulled down over his long black hair, he looks more like a snowboarder than a baseball player. And his awkward throwing motion has confused coaches, reporters, and sports **analysts** (AN-uh-lists) from coast to coast.

Those who once doubted Lincecum's ability to make it in Major League Baseball (MLB) can wonder no more. He is a true star.

Timothy LeRoy Lincecum was born to Chris and Rebecca Lincecum on June 15, 1984, in Bellevue, Washington. Chris Lincecum, who

Tim Lincecum and his father, Chris, hold his 2008 and 2009 Cy Young Awards during a 2010 awards ceremony in San Francisco. When Tim was just five years old, Chris started teaching his son the art of pitching. Tim's father can't make it to all of his games, but they still talk about his pitching on a regular basis.

worked for airplane builder Boeing (BOH-ing), pitched at the high school, junior college, and **semiprofessional** (seh-mee-proh-FEH-shuh-nul) levels. An injury kept him from a career in the major leagues, but he studied the **mechanics** (meh-KAN-iks) of pitching and set out to share what he knew with his sons.

Sean, who is four years older than Tim, got hurt playing football. But Tim's strength, talent, and desire to learn made him the ideal pupil. He and his father spent countless hours perfecting pitches, taping his games, and analyzing each outing. The hard work paid off—even if coaches didn't recognize it at first.

Tim pitching in an Issaquah Little League game in 1995

Tim was smaller than other kids his age. He often spent more time on the bench than on the field. As a ninth grader at Liberty High

Tim got his start in baseball the same way millions of children do: as a Little Leaguer.

School in Renton, Washington, he was just 4 feet 11 inches and weighed 85 pounds. The lack of playing time was frustrating, but Tim simply worked harder. He added weight training to his workouts, and over time, he got stronger—and taller.

By his junior year, Lincecum had grown almost a foot taller and weighed 125 pounds. He made his school's varsity team. He had a great year with the Liberty Patriots, going 4-2 with a 0.73 **ERA** (earned run average). A year later, as a senior, he was named Washington's Gatorade Player of the Year and led his team to the state championship. With a 12-1 record and 183 strikeouts in 91.2 innings, he was an easy selection as Liberty's Most Valuable Player and First Team All-State. In his own way, Lincecum was proving that the best players aren't necessarily the biggest players.

Lincecum played college baseball for the University of Washington, where he became a pitching star. During his junior year, he won the Golden Spikes Award, given annually to college baseball's best player.

A Hit for the Huskies

University of Washington (UW) Coach Ken Knutson (NUT-sun) first met Tim Lincecum at the end of his junior year of high school. A former UW player had suggested the coach check out the kid's arm. At first, Knutson thought it was a joke.

"He was sawed off," Knutson told *Baseball Digest.* "He looked like he was nine."

Then Knutson saw Lincecum pitch. His throws were hard, fast, and accurate. Knutson was so impressed that he offered the pitcher a **scholarship** (SKAH-lur-ship). At about the same time, the Chicago Cubs picked Lincecum in the 2003 Major League Baseball (MLB) **draft.** Lincecum was flattered by the selection, but he still decided to go to college.

He had an outstanding three years with the UW Huskies. In 2004, at the end of his first season, he became the first player named both Pac-10 **Conference** Freshman of the Year and Pac-10 Pitcher of the Year. (The Pac-10, or Pacific-10, Conference is a group of ten teams on the Pacific Coast.) As a sophomore, hitters averaged just .179 against him, and he was an all-conference selection for the second season in a row.

The Cleveland Indians chose Lincecum in the 42nd round of the 2005 MLB draft. At the time, he was playing for the

Lincecum during his college days

University of Washington Huskies Tim Lincecum throws a pitch during an April 2006 game against Brigham Young University.

Harwich (Massachusetts) Mariners, a **collegiate** (kuh-LEE-jet) summer baseball team. His Harwich teammates recall that he turned down Cleveland's signing offer—reportedly $700,000.

"I remember Timmy saying he wanted to sign for enough money so his dad could retire," said Joe Hough, one of Lincecum's closest friends on the team.

Back at the University of Washington, Lincecum started his junior year as one of the nation's top pitching **prospects** (PRAH-spekts)—and he didn't disappoint when he

Harry the Husky hugs one of his favorite University of Washington baseball players.

Lincecum's jersey and number have been painted onto the outfield wall at Husky Ballpark as a tribute to the standout University of Washington pitcher.

threw a school record of 12 wins and 199 strikeouts. The newspaper *Collegiate Baseball* named Lincecum National Player of the Week six times. Tim made the College Baseball Foundation's weekly honor roll seven times.

His statistics were impressive, but his size and unusual pitching style had major league managers worried he'd break down. "[Scouts] talk about my size, or the lack thereof," Lincecum told *ESPN.com* just before the 2006 draft. "So, I have to deal with that. It's something I've had to deal with pretty much my whole life."

Lincecum was such a dominant college pitcher that all eyes were on him as he entered the MLB draft. "My expectations of myself are greater than anyone else's," he told ESPN in June 2006.

Freak or Phenom?

Throughout history, many baseball players have had nicknames. Babe Ruth was the Sultan of Swat. Pete Rose was Charlie Hustle, and Stan Musial was Stan the Man.

Lincecum has a number of nicknames. Some sportswriters have called him Seabiscuit after a racehorse because of how much talent he packs into his small frame. When he pitched in a Cape Cod summer league, his ability to throw strikes earned him the title Doctor Nasty. Others called him The Franchise after he quickly became the face of the Giants.

His most widely used nickname, however, is The Freak. His looks are so youthful that, on more than one occasion in the major leagues, he has been mistaken for a batboy. Even more unusual—or freaky—is the way his slender body violently twists and turns and his long hair flies about as he unleashes the ball.

Lincecum explains his pitching style by saying he propels the ball using every part of his body, from his ankles to his ears. The biggest difference between Lincecum and other hurlers is the length of his stride. According to researchers at the American Sports Medicine Institute, the normal **stride** length for a pitcher is 77 to 87 percent of his height. Lincecum's stride is about seven and a half feet long, or 129 percent of his height.

Not all of his unusual behaviors happen on the field. For example, Lincecum prefers to eat his meals in a squatting position. He never ices his arm. He sings in the dugout, and, unlike many other hurlers, he actually enjoys talking to the media on the days he's pitching.

Catcher Steve Holm played with Lincecum in both the minor and major leagues. He

Lincecum might not be the biggest guy in the major leagues, but he sure can eat! At the In-N-Out hamburger restaurant, this meal, dubbed The Full Lincecum, is his usual order. The meal consists of three Double-Doubles (double cheeseburgers), two orders of fries, and a chocolate-strawberry shake.

brushes off the "freak" label, instead calling Lincecum "a free spirit."

"I think that's what makes him so good," Holm told *Baseball Digest*. "He's so free-spirited, anything negative just washes over him."

Lincecum has both speed and pitch control. During a game against the New York Mets, the scoreboard at Shea Stadium displayed his fastball speed as 98 miles per hour.

Going Pro

Lincecum spent three strong years at the college level. The San Francisco Giants signed him as the tenth overall pick in the 2006 MLB draft for $2 million. Pitchers Max Scherzer, Brandon Morrow, and Brad Lincoln were also drafted in 2006.

Most players spend years working their way through the minor league system, and most never make it to the majors. Lincecum, on the other hand, pitched only 13 times in the minors. He was called up to the majors just 334 days after he was drafted.

Almost from the start, Lincecum has shone as a Giant. During his first full year in

San Francisco, he had an 18-5 record and led the majors with 265 strikeouts. His 95- to 100-mile-per-hour fastballs and wicked curveballs have taken down many of the league's biggest bats.

Lincecum's talent has not gone unnoticed. In 2008 and 2009, he won the Cy Young Award, an honor given to the best pitcher in each league (American and National). He also

Lincecum's French bulldog Cy is a frequent visitor to the Giants clubhouse.

was named to the National League's All-Star team in 2008, 2009, and 2010. As he's proven his value to the team, the Giants have invested more money in their ace. He would earn $8 million in 2010 and $13 million in 2011. He would also be able to earn performance and award bonuses.

The only blotch on Lincecum's early career came in October 2009. During a traffic stop, he was arrested for possession of **marijuana** (mayr-ih-WAH-nah). He went to court, where a judge fined him $513. That was on top of the $150 ticket he had to pay for speeding.

"I'll try not to let this happen again, move forward and continue with my life," an **apologetic** (ah-pah-luh-JEH-tik) Lincecum told those gathered in the courtroom.

Giants' management, team members, and fans hope Lincecum is true to his word. They are counting on him to be the heart—and arm—of their team for years to come.

San Francisco fans greet Lincecum and his World Series champion
Giants teammates during a 2010 parade.

World Champion

Pitching in the World Series is the stuff of boyhood dreams. To be the winning pitcher in two games in a single World Series is the stuff of major league dreams. Lincecum's major league dream became reality in 2010.

His solid-but-not-spectacular pitching in Game 1 contributed to an 11-7 win over the Texas Rangers. Then, on November 1, Lincecum started Game 5 of the series with the chance to win the championship for the San Francisco Giants for the first time ever.

Facing Cliff Lee, one of the league's best left-handers, Lincecum was dominant.

He pitched eight solid innings, collected 10 strikeouts, and gave up just 3 hits on the way to a 3-1 victory.

Lincecum's entire 2010 season was not as rosy. He had a 0-5 record and a 7.82 ERA in August. It was the kind of slump that might have frayed some pitchers' nerves, but Lincecum simply stepped up his training.

Lincecum displays his 2010 World Series championship ring before the Giants took on the St. Louis Cardinals on Opening Day, 2011.

"He made a renewed commitment," pitching coach Dave Righetti told *ESPN*. "I think he just got tired of looking bad. The reason why it worked is he thought this team was going to be good. We all felt there was something at the end of this rainbow."

Now that he has found that shiny World Series trophy at the end of his **postseason** (pohst-SEE-zun) rainbow, Lincecum has a message for those who ever doubted him, his size, or his style: "I think there will always be people out there who say, 'You're never going to do this, you're never going to make it,'" he told the *Seattle Times*. "All I can say to that is, just watch."

Career Statistics

Year	Team	GS	W	L	IP	H	R	ER	HR	BB	K	ERA
2007	Giants	24	7	5	146.1	122	70	65	12	65	150	4.00
2008	Giants	33	18	5	227.0	182	72	66	11	84	265	2.62
2009	Giants	32	15	7	225.1	168	69	62	10	68	261	2.48
2010	Giants	33	16	10	212.1	194	84	81	18	76	231	3.43
Career		122	56	27	811	666	295	274	51	293	907	

GS = Games Started, W = Wins, L = Losses, IP = Innings Pitched, H = Hits, R = Runs, ER = Earned Runs, HR = Home Runs Allowed, BB = Bases on Balls, K = Strikeouts, ERA = Earned Run Average

CHRONOLOGY

1984 Timothy LeRoy Lincecum is born to parents Chris and Rebecca on June 15 in Bellevue, Washington.

2003 Lincecum leads his high school baseball team to the state championship and is named to First Team All-State. He is selected by the Chicago Cubs in the MLB draft but turns down their offer and accepts a scholarship at the University of Washington instead.

2004 He receives conference honors as Freshman of the Year and Pitcher of the Year after his first season at UW.

2005 Lincecum is drafted by the Cleveland Indians, but he refuses their contract offer.

2006 The San Francisco Giants take Lincecum as the tenth pick in the first round of the MLB draft.

2007 His first major league start takes place on May 6; he becomes one of just seven pitchers since 1956 to throw 30 quality starts in his first 40 games.

2008 He is named to the National League All-Star team and caps off his season by winning the Cy Young Award.

2009 Lincecum appears at a charity event called Athletes Against Autism. He is named to the National League All-Star team and becomes the first pitcher in MLB history to win the Cy Young Award in each of his first two full seasons. He also faces charges for possession of marijuana in Washington state.

2010 He leads the Giants to their first World Series title since the franchise moved from New York to San Francisco in 1957, and he is the winning pitcher of Games 1 and 5.

2011 One June 7, Lincecum becomes only the eighth pitcher since 1900 to throw 1,000 strikeouts in his first five seasons in the major leagues.

FIND OUT MORE

Books

Dreier, David Louis. *Baseball: How It Works.* Mankato, MN: Capstone, 2010.

Fitzmaurice, Deanne, and Joan Ryan. *Freak Season: Behind the Scenes with San Francisco Giants Pitcher Tim Lincecum, from Spring Training to the World Series.* San Anselmo, CA: K&D Photography, 2010.

Jacobs, Greg, and Kurt Dolber. *The Everything Kids' Baseball Book: From Baseball History to Player Stats—with Lots of Homerun Fun in Between!* Avon, MA: Adams Media, 2010.

Works Consulted

Associated Press. "For Lincecum, Simple Leads to Spectacular." *The New York Times,* September 21, 2008.

Associated Press. "Lincecum Has a Cy Young and Some Room to Grow." *The New York Times,* March 15, 2009.

Baggarty, Andrew. "Give Lincecum's Dad Credit for Evolution of a Phenom: Chris Lincecum Provided Design and Instruction for His Son Tim's Career." *San Jose Mercury News,* May 25, 2007.

Baggarty, Andrew. "Lincecum Growing Off the Mound, Too." *Oakland (Calif.) Tribune,* August 28, 2008.

Crasnick, Jerry. "Tim Lincecum's Giant-sized Legacy." *ESPN.com,* November 1, 2010.

Curry, Jack. "Giants Leaning Heavily on Skinny Ace." *The New York Times,* September 3, 2009.

Freer, Michael. "Lincecum's Unique Delivery Makes Him Top Prospect." *ESPN.com,* June 2, 2006. http://sports.espn.go.com/ncaa/news/story?id=2453860

Hohler, Bob. "Lincecum's Giants Let Their Hair Down; Ace Brings Looseness—and Cy Youngs." *The Boston Globe,* June 27, 2010.

Killion, Ann. "Giants Welcome the Lincecum Show." *San Jose (Calif.) Mercury News,* May 7, 2007.

Kroichick, Ron. "Tim Lincecum: Big-Time Pitcher in San Francisco: Giants Right-Hander Baffles Hitters with a Fastball Reaching 97 mph and a Devastating Changeup." *Baseball Digest,* October 1, 2008.

Mims, Steve. "Husky's Special K's Stop OSU: UW's Tim Lincecum Fans 16 Beavers to Become Pac-10's All-Time Strikeout Leader." *The Register Guard* (Eugene, Ore.), May 6, 2006.

FIND OUT MORE

Sheinin, Dave. "Lincecum Is a Super 'Freak'; Light Giants Pitcher Heavy on Potential." *The Washington Post,* July 17, 2007.

Stone, Larry. "Quirks and All, Tim Lincecum Quickly Quiets Critics." *Seattle Times,* July 15, 2008.

Verducci, Tom. "How Tiny Tim Became a Pitching Giant." *Sports Illustrated,* July 7, 2008.

On the Internet

Major League Baseball on ESPN
http://espn.go.com/mlb

Official Site of MLB
http://mlb.mlb.com

Official Site of the San Francisco Giants
http://sanfrancisco.giants.mlb.com/

Tim Lincecum Stats, Bio, Photos, Highlights
http://mlb.mlb.com/team/player.jsp?player_id=453311

GLOSSARY

analyst (AN-uh-list)—In sports, a person who talks about all the parts of a game, from players to plays.

apologetic (ah-pah-luh-JEH-tik)—Feeling sorry for one's actions.

collegiate (kuh-LEE-jet)—Related to college.

conference (KON-frunts)—One of several groups of teams within a baseball league.

draft (DRAFT)—The selection of players for professional sports teams.

ERA—Short for earned run average (AV-ridj), this baseball statistic is found by dividing the number of earned runs a pitcher allows by the number of innings pitched, and then multiplying by 9. This gives the average number of runs scored per 9-inning game. Unearned runs (such as those resulting from defensive errors) are not counted in the ERA.

marijuana (mayr-ih-WAH-nah)—The dried leaves and flowers of the hemp plant that are sometimes smoked; smoking marijuana for non-medical reasons is illegal in the United States and many other parts of the world.

mechanics (meh-KAN-iks)—The study of movement, especially when it relates to force or energy.

postseason (pohst-SEE-zun)—After the regular season, a time during which playoff games are held to determine a champion.

prospect (PRAH-spekt)—Someone who seems like a good choice.

scholarship (SKAH-lur-ship)—Money awarded to help pay for college or another type of school.

semiprofessional (seh-mee-proh-FEH-shuh-nul)—Playing a sport for pay, but not on a full-time basis.

stride (STRYD)—The distance traveled in one step.

INDEX